599.72

RHINOS

RHINOS

by Sally M. Walker

photographs by Gerry Ellis

A Carolrhoda Nature Watch Book

 Carolrhoda Books, Inc. / Minneapolis

For David, Erin, Laurie, and Jeff, because they love animals. Also, for all the people who are working to save rhinos from extinction. —S. M. W.

To Anna Merz, who showed us that a single person can make a big difference; to Samia, an abandoned baby rhino who fought for survival and thrived, giving birth to her own calf; and to her baby, Samuel, who gave us hope that wild rhinos will exist in their natural homes forever. —G. E.

Special thanks to Tom Foose of the International Rhino Foundation and Karen Kane of the Rhino Trust for their help with this book.

LIBRARY OF CONGRESS CATALOGING-IN-PUBLICATION DATA

Walker, Sally M.
 Rhinos / by Sally M. Walker ; photographs by Gerry Ellis.
   p.   cm.
 "A Carolrhoda nature watch book."
 Includes index.
 Summary: Describes the physical characteristics, life cycle, behavior, and conservation of rhinos.
  ISBN 1-57505-008-0
  1. Rhinoceroses — Juvenile literature. [1. Rhinoceroses.] I. Ellis, Gerry, ill. II. Title.
 QL737.U63W35 1996
 599.72'8 — dc20   96-228

Manufactured in the United States of America
1 2 3 4 5 6 – JR – 01 00 99 98 97 96

CONTENTS

INTRODUCTION

A mother black rhinoceros and her five-month-old baby calmly chew hay and watch as I walk toward them. Suddenly, a loud noise startles them, and they wheel around and bolt away with surprising speed and grace. At a safe distance, they stop, lower their heads, pick up some hay, and continue eating.

I'm lucky to be able to stand so close to these unusual animals. The reason I can is because they live in Chicago's Brookfield Zoo. Rhinoceroses are among the world's most **endangered** animals and are rarely seen in the wild. If this mother and her son lived in the wild, the terrible truth is they would likely be killed by illegal hunters, called **poachers,** who earn money by selling rhinoceros horns.

Modern rhinoceroses, often called rhinos, are **mammals,** animals who feed their young with their own milk. Mammals such as rhinos who have hooves and an odd number of toes are called **perissodactyls** (puh-RISS-uh-DACK-tuhlz). (Horses, which have one toe, are related to the rhinoceros.)

In the past, about 100 different species, or kinds, of rhinoceroses roamed North America, Europe, Africa, and Asia. Ancient rhino species included hornless rhinos, woolly rhinos, and the largest land mammals ever, a species called Paraceratherium. These huge creatures grew to more than 18 feet (5.5 m) tall and 27 feet (8 m) long!

For about 30 million years, rhinos were the most common land mammal in North America. But they all became **extinct,** or died out, about 5 million years ago. All rhinos in North American zoos come from Africa or Asia, or have ancestors who did.

This ancient rhino species sported two horns side by side.

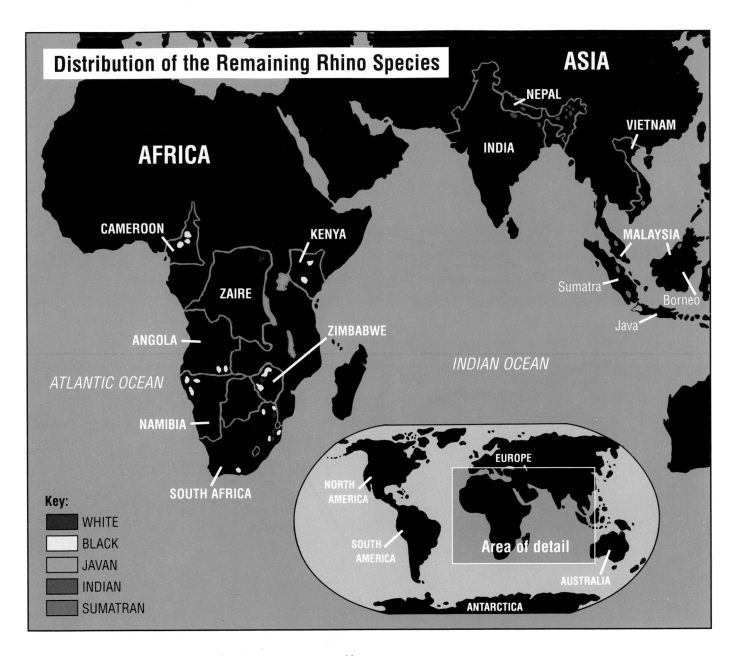

Distribution of the Remaining Rhino Species

ASIA

NEPAL

VIETNAM

INDIA

AFRICA

CAMEROON

KENYA

MALAYSIA

ZAIRE

Sumatra

Borneo

ANGOLA

ZIMBABWE

Java

INDIAN OCEAN

ATLANTIC OCEAN

NAMIBIA

SOUTH AFRICA

Key:
WHITE
BLACK
JAVAN
INDIAN
SUMATRAN

EUROPE

NORTH
AMERICA

Area of detail

SOUTH
AMERICA

AUSTRALIA

ANTARCTICA

Only five species of rhino are still alive, and they too are in danger of extinction. Two species—the white rhino and the black rhino—live in Africa. The other three rhino species—the Indian, the Javan, and the Sumatran—all live in Asia.

White rhinos *(Ceratotherium simum)*, the most common of the five species, live on **savannas**—flat, grassy areas with scattered trees. White rhinos are divided into two subspecies. The southern subspecies *(Ceratotherium simum simum)*, whose population is about 7,000 animals, can be found in several African countries, although most of them live in South Africa. The northern subspecies *(Ceratotherium simum cottoni)* is found only in Garamba National Park, in Zaire. There are only about 30 left in the park. Ten others live in zoos around the world.

Black rhinos *(Diceros bicornis)* usually live in wooded areas with low shrubs and small trees. In the past, black rhinos sometimes roamed the edges of savannas as well. Unfortunately, wandering across open land made them easy targets for poachers, and their numbers have dwindled from about 65,000 in the early 1970s to about 2,500 in 1996.

*A **white rhinoceros** (Ceratotherium simum)*

Indian rhinos *(Rhinoceros unicornis)* prefer to live in marshy places, especially in tall grass near rivers. They can also live on drier grassy plains or in hilly country. In the past, Indian rhinos roamed across much of northern India. But they are quickly being squeezed off the land by poachers and farmers who are clearing the land to grow crops. Most of the world's 2,000 remaining Indian rhinos live in two areas: northeastern India and nearby Nepal.

Left: *A black rhinoceros* (Diceros bicornis)
Below: *An Indian rhinoceros* (Rhinoceros unicornis)

A Javan rhinoceros (Rhinoceros sondaicus)

Javan rhinos *(Rhinoceros sondaicus)* once roamed throughout the lush forests that cover the Indonesian islands of Java and Sumatra and parts of Southeast Asia. Javan rhinos are good climbers and have been sighted in areas with hills measuring more than a mile (1.6 km) high. Like Indian rhinos, Javan rhinos have also been pushed off the land as more people have settled there to farm. Most Javan rhinos live in Ujung Kulon National Park, on the western tip of Java. There are only about 50 of them left in the park. Another group of fewer than 20 Javan rhinos lives in southern Vietnam.

Sumatran rhinos *(Dicerorhinus sumatrensis)* are forest dwellers as well. In the past, they have roamed the Indonesian islands of Borneo and Sumatra, northeastern India, and much of Southeast Asia. That area has since been reduced to small parts of the Malay Peninsula, Borneo, and Sumatra. Sumatran rhinos are the best climbers of the rhino species; some of the slopes they climb are so steep that a person would have to climb them on hands and knees. Tracks of Sumatran rhinos, like those of Javan rhinos, have been found on hills higher than a mile. There are about 400 Sumatran rhinos alive. But although they number more than Javan rhinos, Sumatran rhinos are considered more endangered, because poaching of the Sumatrans has increased.

Together, there are approximately 12,000 rhinos left in the wild—many of whom live in national parks or in **sanctuaries,** privately owned and protected areas. An additional 1,000 rhinos live in zoos around the world.

A Sumatran rhinoceros (Dicerorhinus sumatrensis)

PHYSICAL CHARACTERISTICS

In addition to being perissodactyls, rhinos belong to a group of mammals called **pachyderms** (PAK-ih-durms). The word *pachyderm* comes from two Greek words: *pachys*, meaning "thick," and *derma*, meaning "skin." Elephants and hippopotamuses are also pachyderms.

All five species of rhinos have large, barrel-shaped bodies covered with thick, gray skin. A rhinoceros's skin may be from 0.5 to 0.75 inches (1–2 cm) thick.

In the 1500s and 1600s, many people believed the rhino's skin was like armor. But despite its thickness, rhino skin can be pierced easily by knives, spears, or bullets. If you look closely, you'll see that this black rhino has a sore on its left side. These sores are common among black rhinos.

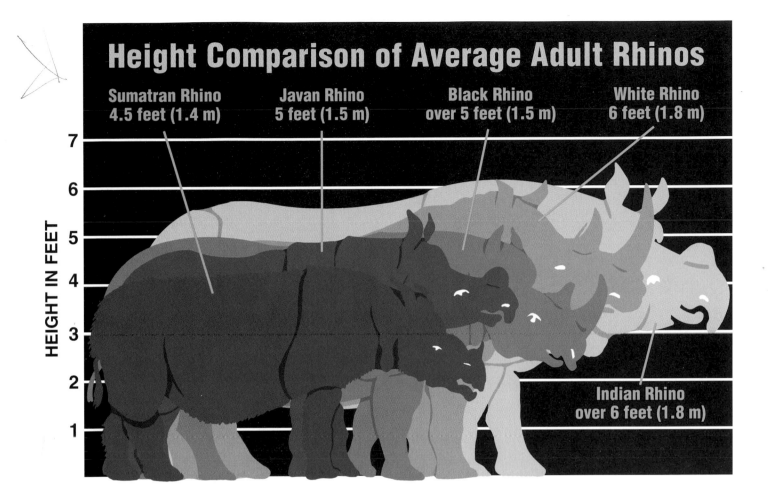

Height Comparison of Average Adult Rhinos

HEIGHT IN FEET

Sumatran Rhino
4.5 feet (1.4 m)

Javan Rhino
5 feet (1.5 m)

Black Rhino
over 5 feet (1.5 m)

White Rhino
6 feet (1.8 m)

Indian Rhino
over 6 feet (1.8 m)

Rhinos vary in size from species to species. Indian and white rhinos are the largest. Indian rhinos can grow as tall as 6.5 feet (2 m) at the shoulder, while white rhinos average 5 to 6 feet (1.5–1.8 m) tall. Javan and black rhinos are usually smaller and average about 5 feet (1.5 m) tall. Sumatran rhinos seem tiny when compared to the other species. Full grown, they are only 4 feet (1.2 m) tall and weigh about 1,500 pounds (681 kg).

White and Indian rhinos are the species' heavyweights, weighing in at about 4,500 pounds (2,043 kg), three times the weight of a Sumatran rhino! Adult Javans usually reach about 2,500 pounds (1,135 kg). Black rhinos tip the scales at 2,000 to 3,000 pounds (908–1,362 kg). Males of all rhino species, called **bulls,** are larger than females, or **cows.**

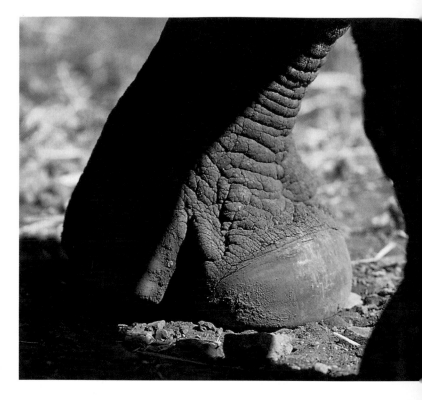

Top: *Most of a rhino's weight is supported on its large center toes.*
Bottom: *A rhino's ears are alert for the sounds of approaching danger.*

All rhinos have three toes on each foot, but the large center toe is the one that bears most of the rhinoceros's weight. The sole of the foot is a hard, rubbery pad. Even though they appear clumsy, a rhinoceros's legs are strong and powerful. When frightened, a rhino can turn around and run faster than you could. Rhinos can gallop for short distances at speeds of 25 to 31 miles per hour (40–50 km/hr). If a rhino is angry or irritated, it may charge at whatever is bothering it—horns first!

Perhaps because their eyesight isn't too keen, rhinos have developed excellent hearing and smelling to help them sense danger. First they swivel their ears and pinpoint the direction a sound is coming from. Then they use their noses to help them decide if it's something they need to worry about.

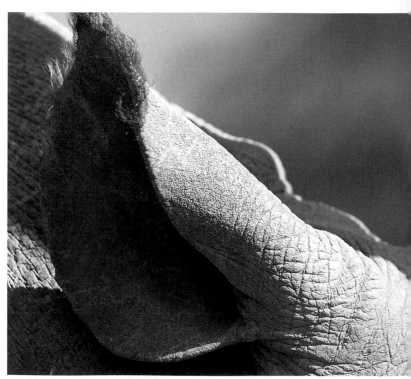

14

Rhinos sharpen their horns by scraping them against trees or rocks.

Horns are the species' most recognizable characteristic. In fact, the name *rhinoceros* comes from two Greek words: *rhino,* which means "nose," and *keras,* which means "horn." All rhinos have at least one horn.

Rhino horns are different from the antlers and horns of other mammals. First of all, a rhino horn grows on the animal's nose rather than on the top of its head. It grows up from the skin and is supported beneath the skin by a bony knob on the rhino's skull. The knob is larger in the Asian rhinoceros species, so their horns don't break off as easily.

Rhino horns are also different from other animals' horns because they don't have a pith, or spongy, bony center. Rhino horns are made of **keratin,** the same substance that forms hooves, hair, and fingernails. If you looked at a rhino horn through a microscope, you would see that it consists of separate hairlike strands that are packed tightly together. Because the keratin fibers are so closely packed, rhino horn is hard like other kinds of horn—hard enough that a charging rhino can poke a hole in a car door! If a rhino's horn breaks or splits apart, it tends to peel off in strands.

Although a horn makes a rhino look rather peculiar to us, the rhino finds it very useful. A frightened or angry rhino can use its horn to toss its enemies—such as hyenas, lions, and even people—into the air. They also use it to joust with other rhinos in tests of strength. If a fight between rhinos becomes serious, a rhino will thrust its horn upward and stab its opponent.

Rhinos' horns can also come in handy at mealtimes. They use them to pull down or break tree limbs in order to reach the leaves to eat. During very dry weather, when many plants have died, rhinos use their horns as shovels to dig for roots or water. Sometimes a horn gets broken or torn off, but it grows back.

It's hard to tell if these two black rhinos are just scuffling to determine who is stronger or if they are really trying to hurt each other.

No two rhinos' horns are exactly alike. The back horn of the rhino on the right is longer than the front horn. This suggests that its front horn broke off some time ago and is in the process of growing back.

The number and size of the horns on a rhino's nose is a good way to tell rhino species apart. Javan and Indian rhinos have only one horn; Sumatran, white, and black rhinos have two horns. White and black rhinos have the longest horns. A white rhino's front horn often grows to 6 feet (1.8 m). The longest white rhino horn on record was over 6.5 feet long (2 m)—longer than a tall man! A black rhino's front horn usually grows to be a little over 4 feet (1.2 m) long—about the size of an average 8- or 9-year-old child. The back horn of white and black rhinos is normally shorter than the front horn, perhaps only 14 to 16 inches (36–41 cm) long. Asian rhinos have much shorter horns. The front horn of a Sumatran rhino can be anywhere from 10 to 31 inches (26–79 cm) long, and the back horn may be only a short nub. An Indian rhino horn is usually from 8 to 24 inches (20–61 cm) long. The Javan rhino has the shortest horn of all. A bull's horn may reach only 10 to 10.5 inches (25–27 cm). Javan cows often have only a small knob.

The skin of the black rhino (top) and the white rhino (bottom) are very similar.

The pattern of folds on a rhino's skin is another way to identify its species. The African species don't have as many folds in their skin as the Asian species do. The folds they do have are in the lower neck area, along the tops of their legs, and near the rump. The skin of white and black rhinos has a crinkly, leathery appearance but is fairly smooth to the touch. And surprisingly, the skin on their snout and around their eyes feels just like the soft skin between a horse's nostrils—almost exactly like velvet!

An Indian rhino's skin folds across its shoulders, the top of its rump, and near the base of its tail. It has a partial fold near its neck. What makes the Indian rhino easy to identify are the knobby bumps that cover much of its body. These bumps make an Indian rhino's skin look as if it were bolted together.

A Javan rhino has a large fold of skin all the way across its neck and shoulders, as well as a fold across the base of its tail. Its skin has a crisscross pattern of wrinkles that looks somewhat scaly. It does not have bumps like the Indian rhino.

The Sumatran rhino is probably the easiest to identify. In addition to the large fold of skin across its shoulders, its whole body is covered with long, dark hair, which is especially thick when the rhino is young. It is the only hairy rhino species. The other four species have hair only along their ears, on the tips of their tails, and as eyelashes.

Indian rhinos (above) *are easily identified by the deep creases and large knobs in their skin.* *Sumatran rhinos* (left) *are hairy.*

Rhinos have 24 to 34 teeth, depending on their species. The exact kind of teeth they have is suited to the kinds of food they eat. All rhinos are herbivores, animals who eat plants, but they don't all eat the same ones. Savanna grasses are different from the tall, twiggy shrubs and trees that grow in forests.

All rhinos have 12 to 14 pairs of **molars,** large, ridged teeth located in the back of the mouth. Molars are used for grinding up plants. The three Asian species also have **incisors** (in-SY-zers), sharp teeth in the front of the mouth used for nipping grass and leaves. African rhinos don't have incisors. Only Sumatran rhinos have a sharp, cone-shaped **canine tooth** on each side of their lower jaw. Scientists suspect that they do not use their canine teeth for eating at all, but for slashing opponents during fights.

canine teeth

A Sumatran rhino shows its canine teeth.

A white rhino holds its head low to the ground even when it's not eating. To lift its heavy head to look around, it uses the powerful muscles that make up the hump on its neck.

Rhinos eat by grabbing plants with their lips and pulling them into their mouths. The way they do this depends on the kind of plants they eat and the shape of their upper lip. White rhinos have a wide, square upper lip, perfectly suited for ripping off large clumps of grass. In fact, it's this wide upper lip that gave the white rhinoceros its name. The "white" in its name has nothing to do with its color—white and black rhinos are pretty much the same shade of gray. "White" is really a mistranslation of the Dutch word *wijde*, which means "wide." (Dutch was one of the languages spoken by early European settlers in Africa.)

Black, Sumatran, and Javan rhinos are all considered to be browsers, animals whose normal diet consists of tender shoots, twigs, and leaves. These three species have a pointed upper lip called a **prehensile** (pree-HENT-sill) lip. Something is prehensile if it can grab and hold on to an object. (Your fingers are a good example.) A rhino with a prehensile lip wraps the lip around leaves and twigs, rips them off, and pulls them into its mouth. It can also use its lip to pluck fruit from a tree, pick up fallen fruit from the ground, or tear up long grasses.

Hungry Sumatran and Javan rhinos have been observed "walking down" young trees. To do this, a rhino walks toward a tree until it is bent over and trapped between the rhino's front legs. When the leaves are within reach, the rhino eats them, along with any tasty fruit that may be growing on the tree. Some rhinos are strong enough to walk down trees with trunks as thick as 3 to 4 inches (8–10 cm).

Sumatran (left) and black rhinos (above) have a prehensile upper lip that works like a small finger.

Although poachers are the biggest danger for Indian rhinos, farmers also pose a risk. The areas where Indian rhinos live are being cleared to make farmland, such as this tea plantation, and they are being killed by farmers protecting their crops from the hungry animals.

Indian rhinos are considered grazers, animals that eat mostly grasses. They have a partially prehensile lip, which they fold up out of the way while they are grazing. They also eat fruit, water plants, bamboo shoots, leaves, and shrubs, and that is where their prehensile lip comes in handy. Unfortunately, Indian rhinos also like to eat young rice plants, corn, lentils, and potatoes—crops grown by local farmers. Understandably, this makes the farmers angry.

23

DIET AND DAILY ROUTINE

It's difficult to observe rhinos in the wild, so it's hard to know exactly how much food they eat per day. Rhinos in zoos are fed hay mixed with grains, vitamins, and minerals to keep them healthy. They eat about 1 to 2 percent of their body weight per day, or 45 to 90 pounds (20–41 kg) for white rhinos and 25 to 50 pounds (11–23 kg) for Javans.

Unlike zoo rhinos, rhinos in the wild must search for their food. How large an area a rhino roams depends on how much food is available. When food is plentiful, the area can be small, only a few square miles. If food is scarce, a feeding area must be larger, sometimes 6 square miles (16 km²) or more. Browsers often roam farther than grazers, because the shrubs browsers enjoy don't grow close together the way grasses do.

Rhinos spend almost half their lives eating. They usually eat during the cooler parts of the day—in the evening, at night, and in the early morning.

The hottest part of each day is spent resting and trying to stay cool. Approximately one-third of a rhino's day is spent resting or sleeping. Rhinos are sound sleepers. They may lie on their side with their legs stretched out, but more often they lie with their legs gathered beneath them, head upright, with their chin resting on the ground. Like horses, rhinos can also sleep standing up.

A black rhino finds some shade to protect it from the midday heat.

A black rhino goes for a drink.

All rhinos live in warm places, so they need water regularly. They drink from 15 to 25 gallons (57–95 l.) of water a day. Although rhinos can go several days without water, they prefer to stay in an area where they can drink daily. They sometimes chew succulent, or water-filled, plants if they can't get to water, but rhinos will walk from 5 to 15 miles (8–24 km) a day in order to drink. In times of very dry weather, they will dig to reach water that flows underground.

Rhinos often plop into the water and rest or sleep in it. They also splash around and swim (particularly Indian rhinos, who live near rivers). Rhinos can't sweat like we do, so this helps them stay cool.

Another way rhinos stay cool is to **wallow,** or roll around, in cool, wet mud. When it dries, the muddy covering protects them against sunburn and makes it more difficult for **parasites** and insects to bite them. If no mud is available, a rhino will wallow in the dust, which probably provides some protection and gives the rhino a nice back scratch.

Mud and dust don't keep all biting pests away, though. That's why when it's time to "debug," certain birds are rhinos' best friends. In Africa, the oxpecker, sometimes called the tick bird, lands on a rhino and then works its way around the rhino's body, eating ticks. In Asia, mynah birds help out Indian rhinos the same way. Rhinos don't even seem to mind when the birds peck inside their ears or around their nostrils. Oxpeckers also act as an alarm system. When danger approaches, the birds fly up into the air and squawk loudly, alerting the rhino of possible trouble.

Top: *A white rhino cools off in the mud.*
Bottom: *Oxpeckers at work*

A rhino travels specific routes to its feeding areas and the nearest water hole. Walking to and fro each day wears a grooved path that may be as wide as 20 inches (51 cm) and as deep as 14 inches (36 cm). Rhino paths that cut through heavy plant growth are like low, green tunnels. Paths leading to water holes are considered public property, and rhinos share them with other rhinos. However, paths to sleeping and feeding areas are considered private.

Unless a cow has a calf, she doesn't usually mind being near other cows or young adult rhinos. Bulls are more solitary. When they meet, they test each other's strength by horn wrestling and charging into each other's shoulders. This establishes which bull is the strongest. That bull will occupy a dominant, or higher, social position. As long as the weaker bull doesn't challenge the dominant one, a meeting may not lead to a fight. In places where the amount of available space is limited, like a national park or zoo, rhinos tolerate the presence of others.

Two black rhino bulls eye each other.

29

CALLS, SIGNALS, AND SIGNS

Rhinos communicate using a wide range of sounds and body language. If a dominant bull making his daily rounds meets another bull, he growls and may curl his tail up over his back as a sign that he is upset. Unless he's looking for trouble, the other (most likely younger) male chirps at the stronger bull as if to say, "Relax, I know who's in charge." If a fight erupts, both adults roar and grunt.

Although a baby rhino's call is much quieter than a bull's, it is sure to bring a quick response from its mother. It may whine to grab her attention or squeal if it is afraid. Then mom comes running.

Scientists called zoologists, who study animal life, recently learned that rhinos also use a "silent" call to communicate with each other. Like whales' songs, these **infrasonic** sounds are below the range of sounds that humans can hear and can travel long distances.

A young black rhino calls out to its mother.

30

Rhinos announce their presence by leaving behind urine (left) *and dung* (above).

Not all rhino communication involves sound. Like many animals, a rhino bull lets others know the boundaries of his **home range**—the area in which he lives—by spraying urine on bushes, trees, grass, and rocks. African rhino bulls patrolling the borders of their home ranges spray every few minutes. Zoologists aren't sure if all male urine spraying is range marking. It's possible that it may be a kind of identifying mark left to say, "Hey, I've been here!" whether they're in their own home range or not.

Rhinos also mark their presence by defecating, or eliminating solid waste, in communal **dung** heaps. Over time, these piles may reach 3 feet (0.9 m) high and 16 feet (4.9 m) across. A rhino's excellent sense of smell enables it to tell rhino neighbors and strangers apart by the scent of their dung. That way, a rhino can keep track of who is around. And it seems it's just as important to be smelled as it is to smell others. Wildlife observers have seen white rhinos in full gallop suddenly stop when they reach a communal dung heap, defecate, and then take off running again!

LIFE CYCLE

When a female rhino is in **estrus,** the time when she is able to become pregnant, she sprays urine and makes a whistling sound. The scent of her urine lets bulls know she is ready to mate. Cows begin to experience estrus at about 3 years of age, but they may not have their first baby for several more years. Bulls are able to reproduce at about 7 to 9 years of age.

Courting rhinos don't murmur sweet nothings into each other's ear. Rhino courtship is noisy and sometimes even violent. Snorting, squealing, puffing, roaring, and whistling are some of the sounds courting rhinos make. Cows have been known to attack courting bulls and injure them with their horns.

In this photo, the courting black rhinos seem to be nuzzling each other gently. But the bull's bloody face is evidence of the violent side of mating.

Just before mating, a bull lays its head across the cow's back. During the next day or so, the bull may mount and mate with the cow several times. But after that, they both go their separate ways. Rhinos do not remain together as a family, and the bull does not help to raise their baby, called a **calf.**

Gestation, the time a calf needs to develop inside the mother before it is born, varies slightly among the five species. Gestation averages 15 months for black rhinos and 16 months for white and Indian rhinos. Sumatran and Javan rhinos are so hard to find that it's almost impossible to study them. But based on the animals' size and weight, zoologists think that a Javan rhino's gestation period is about 16 months too. For Sumatran rhinos, it is probably 15 months.

Mating rhinos remain together only a few days.

A rhino cow gives birth standing up and delivers one calf. Twins are very rare. Shortly before her baby is born, a cow often gets irritable. Female rhinos in zoos, who are normally calm and friendly with their keepers, sometimes become violent in the days before the baby's birth. They resume their gentle manner within days, sometimes only hours, after giving birth.

In the wild, a female usually hides when she is about to give birth. She and the calf remain alone for several days. The mother probably does this for the calf's protection, since bulls sometimes attack newborn calves.

Even at birth, all rhino babies are pretty big, measuring about 2 feet (0.6 m) tall. However, white and Indian rhino newborns weigh 100 to 150 pounds (45–68 kg), while newborn black calves weigh 60 to 90 pounds (27–41 kg). (We know very little about the weights of newborn Javan and Sumatran rhinos.)

Rhinos are born with a smooth, flat, oval plate on their nose. At about 5 weeks of age, a horn will start to grow there. Rhino calves have the same folds in their skin as adults do. They also may have some hair on their bodies, which falls out as they grow older (unless they are Sumatran rhinos).

A one-month-old black rhino

Baby rhinos struggle to their feet as soon as 10 minutes after birth. Wobbly at first, they are fairly steady on their legs within a few hours. Right away, calves search for one of their mother's two nipples and begin nursing. They nurse often and for several minutes at a time, so a mother rhino must be able to produce a lot of milk. For example, an Indian rhino cow produces from 34 to 44 pints (16–21 l.) of milk per day to meet her baby's nutritional needs. That's enough milk for an entire class of 30 kindergartners!

Baby rhinos gain weight rapidly—as much as 4.5 to 6.5 pounds (2–3 kg) a day. Calves nurse for about a year and slowly add solid food to their diet. By the end of that year, the baby will be about ten times heavier than it was at birth. In zoos, calves as young as 2 weeks old have been seen nibbling plants, but they don't usually eat them regularly until they are a few months old.

This calf never strays far from its food—mother's milk.

Rhino mothers are very protective of their babies and always keep them close by. Healthy adult rhinos don't really have any **predators,** or animals that hunt them (except humans), but baby rhinos are attacked by hyenas, tigers, and occasionally lions. In times of danger, a mother rhino will turn sideways so that her body blocks the predator's path to her baby. If several white rhino cows and calves are in a group and danger arises, the cows arrange themselves in a circle, rumps toward the center and horns pointing outward, around the group of calves. Faced with the points of so many horns, a smart predator will think twice about attacking.

A protective black rhino mother leads her young calf.

Black rhino mothers always make their calves travel behind them. Many zoologists believe this is because they live in a wooded, shrub-filled **habitat,** or area. A predator can easily hide in the brush and jump out and attack a baby rhino before it is aware of the danger. But an alert mother rhino walking ahead of her baby is able to handle any surprise attackers that might leap into her path.

In contrast, white rhino calves always walk in front of their mothers. Again, habitat may determine this behavior. As the mother moves along behind her calf, she has a good view of any predators who may be sneaking across the open savanna. Indian rhino calves seem to take advantage of both strategies. Very young Indian rhinos tend to follow their mothers. As they get older and larger, they shift position and the youngsters travel in front.

Calves remain with their mothers until they are about 2 to 3 years old. Sometimes they stay together longer. Females can give birth every 2 to 3 years, but if she is still caring for a calf, a cow in the wild may wait up to 5 years before mating again. When a new calf is born, the cow drives the older calf away. Over a natural life span, a rhino may have as many as 10 or 11 calves.

After leaving their mothers, young rhinos frequently join up with one or more other rhinos, usually of the same sex and about the same age. Sometimes they will tag along with an **aunt,** an older, childless female. They travel around together until they are ready to establish their own home ranges, usually by the time they are 5.

Rhinos in zoos have lived into their forties. Left to die of natural causes in the wild, they may live longer. Unfortunately, most rhinos in the wild are killed before they have the chance to live out a natural lifetime.

This "baby" black rhino is nearly old enough to live on its own. But its mother still walks in front.

THE KILLING MUST STOP

If rhinos become extinct in our lifetimes, it will be due entirely to human activity. Over the years, we have killed rhinos for their horns and destroyed their habitats to create fields for agriculture and to supply lumber for the timber industry. Tens of thousands more rhinos were killed by sport hunters before rhino hunting became illegal.

During the past 20 years, however, most rhinos have been killed when poachers have cut out their horns. Rhino horn has been an ingredient in traditional medicines for hundreds of years and is still used in China, Taiwan, and Korea. As recently as 1992, more than 1,100 pounds (499 kg) of rhino horn were used each year as a fever remedy. Rhino conservation groups estimate that there are 26,000 to 36,000 pounds (11,804–16,344 kg) more rhino horn in illegal stockpiles in China and Taiwan.

Those figures alone account for about 17,000 to 24,000 rhinos—roughly twice the number still alive around the world.

Rhino horn has also been in great demand in northern Yemen, where it is carved into handles for fancy daggers, which are given to young Yemeni men as a symbol of becoming adults. During the 1970s, an average of 16,000 pounds (7,264 kg) of rhino horn were sold there each year. Thankfully, sales of the daggers have slowed since then.

An international law bans the trade of rhino horn. Unfortunately, rhino-horn dealers are willing to break the law and risk getting caught because they can find buyers willing to pay up to $30,000 per pound—$45,000 for an average, 1.5 pound (0.7 kg) Indian rhino horn. That's almost five times the price of a pound of gold.

A ranger examines white rhino horns taken from poachers in South Africa.

Catching poachers and dealers is one step in the fight to save rhinos from extinction. Another step is to refuse to buy goods from countries that don't crack down hard on the use of rhino products. In September 1994, President Clinton announced that the United States would no longer buy certain wildlife products from Taiwan. The new policy was in effect until June 1995, when Taiwan showed proof it was stopping the use and trade of rhino products.

Educating people about rhinoceroses and the seriousness of their situation is a crucial step in saving rhinos. Even though it may be difficult, people must learn to use other materials for dagger handles and to treat illnesses with aspirin or other substances that reduce fevers.

LOOKING AHEAD

The future survival of rhinos depends on what we do now to protect them. Although one rhino was killed in 1994, the Javan rhino population in Ujung Kulon National Park has been doing fairly well. Plans are being made to fence in one area of the park to create a sanctuary that will keep the remaining rhinos even safer.

A dehorned white rhino

Even though national parks are patrolled and guarded, poaching in the national parks of Nepal, India, South Africa, and Zimbabwe is still a very serious problem. Some African countries have tried to stop poachers by capturing rhinos and sawing off their horns. This is a very expensive undertaking, because rhinos' horns grow back again. Tragically, when there aren't enough rangers to patrol an area constantly, poachers kill dehorned rhinos anyway. (Even the stub of a horn is valuable.) And **dehorning** might make it harder for rhino mothers to protect their babies from predators. However, a combination of methods—hiring more rangers *and* dehorning rhinos—may be effective at saving them.

Left: *Samia, a black rhino cow, is not afraid around humans. She was raised from birth on the Ngare Sergoi Rhino Sanctuary in Kenya by the owner of the sanctuary, Anna Merz.*
Below: *In Ngare Sergoi, the rhino rules.*

The safest places for rhinos seem to be sanctuaries. These areas are heavily patrolled and surrounded by electric fences to keep poachers out, so rhinos are able to live and breed in safety.

Zoos are also actively working to save rhinos from extinction. The Species Survival Plan is one program that helps endangered species by breeding them in captivity. The mother and baby black rhinos at the Brookfield Zoo are part of this program. Zoologists hope to learn more about rhino reproduction to make captive breeding programs even more effective. Someday maybe the world will be safe enough to release some young rhinos back into the wild.

The Minnesota Zoo is helping to save Javan rhinos in the wild by participating in the Adopt-a-Park Program. The zoo sends money (donated by visitors to the zoo) directly to Ujung Kulon National Park, where it is used to buy supplies and equipment to protect rhinos and to pay rangers.

Conservationists estimate it will cost $60 to $100 million over the next five years to save Asian rhinos, and even more to save African rhinos. This money will also help save rhino habitats and all the creatures who share them. We must find ways to make this happen. The rhinoceros's future is in our hands.

For more information about rhino conservation, write:

The Rhino Trust
4045 North Massachusetts Avenue
Portland, OR 97219

The International Rhino Foundation
14000 International Road
Cumberland, OH 43732

GLOSSARY

aunt: a calfless adult female rhino that keeps company with one or more immature rhinos

bull: an adult male rhinoceros

calf: a baby rhinoceros

canine tooth: one of two sharp teeth near the front of the lower jaw in Sumatran rhinos

cow: an adult female rhinoceros

dehorning: the process of cutting off a rhino's horn

dung: an animal's solid waste

endangered: at risk of losing all members of a species forever

estrus: the period during which a female rhino can become pregnant

extinct: having no members of a species left alive

gestation: the period of development before birth

habitat: the type of area where something lives, such as a forest

home range: the area in which an animal eats, roams, and breeds

incisor: a tooth near the front of the upper jaw in Asian rhino species that is used for cutting grass and leaves

infrasonic: too low for humans to hear

keratin: a protein that makes up rhino horn and human fingernails

mammal: one of a group of animals who feed their young with milk from their own bodies

molar: a large, flat tooth in the back of rhinos' mouths that is used for grinding food.

pachyderm: one of a group of animals with hooves and thick skin, including rhinos, elephants, and pigs

parasite: an organism that lives on or in another organism and usually causes its host harm

perissodactyl: one of a group of animals with hooves and an odd number of toes, including rhinos and horses

poachers: people who hunt illegally

predator: an animal who kills other animals for food

prehensile: able to grasp something

sanctuary: a privately owned area fenced and guarded to protect the wildlife inside

savanna: a flat, grassy area with only a few trees

wallow: to roll around, usually in mud

47

INDEX